Practical Machine Learning
A New Look at Anomaly Detection

Ted Dunning and Ellen Friedman

Beijing · Cambridge · Farnham · Köln · Sebastopol · Tokyo

Practical Machine Learning

by Ted Dunning and Ellen Friedman

Printed in the United States of America.

Published by O'Reilly Media, Inc., 1005 Gravenstein Highway North, Sebastopol, CA 95472.

O'Reilly books may be purchased for educational, business, or sales promotional use. Online editions are also available for most titles (*http://safaribooksonline.com*). For more information, contact our corporate/institutional sales department: 800-998-9938 or *corporate@oreilly.com*.

Editor: Mike Loukides

June 2014:   First Edition

Revision History for the First Edition:

2014-05-14:   First release

2014-08-08:   Second release

See *http://oreilly.com/catalog/errata.csp?isbn=9781491911600* for release details.

ISBN: 978-1-491-91160-0

[LSI]

Table of Contents

CHAPTER 1

Looking Toward the Future

Everyone loves a mystery, and at the heart of it, that's what anomaly detection is—spotting the unusual, catching the fraud, discovering the strange activity. Anomaly detection has a wide range of useful applications, from banking security to natural sciences to medicine to marketing. Anomaly detection carried out by a machine-learning program is actually a form of artificial intelligence. With the ever-increasing volume of data and the new types of data, such as sensor data from an increasingly large variety of objects that needs to be considered, it's no surprise that there also is a growing interest in being able to handle more decisions automatically via machine-learning applications. But in the case of anomaly detection, at least some of the appeal is the excitement of the chase itself.

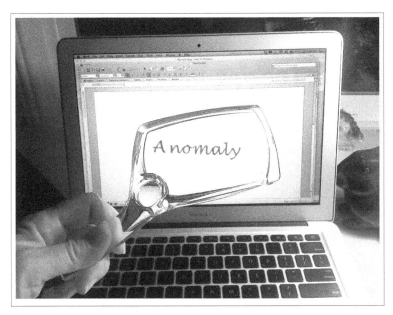

Figure 1-1. Finding anomalies is the detective work of machine learning.

When are anomaly-detection methods a good choice? Unlike fictional detective stories, in anomaly detection, you may not have a clear suspect to search for, and you may not even know what the "crime" is. In fact, one way to think about when to turn to anomaly detection is this: *Anomaly detection is about finding what you don't know to look for.*

You are searching for anomalies, but you don't know what their characteristics will be. If you did, you could use a different form of machine learning, called classification, or you would just write specific rules to find the anomalies. But that's not generally where you start.

Classification is a form of supervised learning where you have examples of each *kind* of thing you are looking for. You apply a learning algorithm to these examples to build a model that can use features of new data to classify them into categories that represent each kind of data of interest. When you have examples of normal and some number of abnormal situations, classifers can help you mark new situations as normal or abnormal. Even when you know about some kinds of anomalies, it is always good to keep an eye out for new kinds that you don't know about. That is where anomaly detection is applied.

So you use the unsupervised-learning approach of anomaly detection when you don't know exactly what you are looking for. Anomaly detection is a discovery process to help you figure out what is going on and what you need to look for. The anomaly-detection program must discover interesting patterns or connections in the data itself, and the detector does this by first identifying the most important aspect of anomaly detection: *finding what is normal.* Once your model does that, your machine-learning program can then spot outliers, in other words, data that falls outside of what is normal.

Anomalies are defined not by their own characteristics, but in contrast to what is normal. You may not know what the anomalies will look like, but you can build a system to detect them in contrast to what you've discovered and defined as being a normal pattern. Note that normal in this context includes all of the anomalies that you already know about and have accounted for using a classifier. The outliers are only those events that don't match what you already know. Consider this way to think about the problem: anomaly in this context just means different than expected—it does not refer to desirable or undesirable. You may know of certain types of events that are somewhat unusual and require attention, perhaps certain failures in a system. If these occur sufficiently often to be well characterized, you can use a classifier to catalog them as problems of a particular type. That's a somewhat different goal than true anomaly detection where you are looking for events that are rare relative to what is expected and that often are surprising, or at least undefined ahead of time.

Together, anomaly detection and classification make for a useful pair when it comes to finding a solution to real-world problems. Anomaly detection is used first—in a discovery phase—to help you figure out what is going on and what you need to look for. You could use the anomaly-detection model to spot outliers, then set up an efficient classification model to assign new examples to the categories you've already identified. You then update the anomaly detector to consider these new examples as normal and repeat the process. This idea is shown in Figure 1-2 as one way to use anomaly detection.

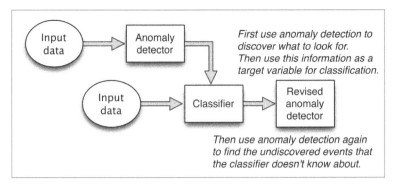

Figure 1-2. Use anomaly detection when you don't know what to look for. Sometimes this discovery process makes a useful preliminary stage to define the categories of interest for a classifier.

Anomaly detection, like classification, is not new, but recently there has been an increased interest in using it. Fortunately, there also are new approaches to carrying it out effectively in practical settings; much more accurate and sophisticated methods are now available. Some of the biggest changes have to do with being able to handle anomaly detection at huge scale, in real time. We will describe some approaches that can help, especially when using a realtime distributed file system. We will focus particularly on approaches that have demonstrated, practical, and simple implementations.

The move from specialized academic research to methods that are useful for practical machine learning is happening in response to more than just an increase in the *volume* of available data—there is also a great increase in *new types* of data. For example, many new forms of sensors are being deployed. Smart meters monitor energy usage in businesses and residential settings, reporting back every few minutes. This information can be used individually or looked at as a group from a particular geographical location.

Figure 1-3. This wall of smart meters reports a granular view of energy usage for a utility company. Sensor data is becoming a huge source of valuable information that can be analyzed through machine learning techniques such as anomaly detection.

Industrial equipment such as drilling rigs and manufacturing tools use sensors to report on a wide range of parameters. The advances in medical device sensors are astounding. Radio-frequency identification (RFID) tags are also commonplace on merchandise in retail stores, in warehouses, or even on your cat. Data provided by these sensors and other sources range from simple identification signals to complex measurements of temperature, pressure, vibrations, and more.

How can reporting from all these interconnected objects be used? Collectively, these objects begin to make up the Internet of Things (IoT). Relationships between objects and people, between objects and other objects, conditions in the present, and histories of their condition over time can be monitored and stored for future analysis, but doing so is quite a challenge. However, the rewards are also potentially enormous. That's where machine learning and anomaly detection can provide a huge benefit.

Analysts predict that the number of interconnected devices in the Internet of Things will reach the tens of billions less than a decade from this writing. Machine-learning techniques will be critical to our understanding of what the signals from devices are telling us.

As we collect and analyze more data from sensors, we achieve a more granular view of how our systems are functioning, which in turn gives us the opportunity for a greater awareness of when things change for better or for worse. Not only is there a growing need for more accurate anomaly detection, there is also a growing desire for new and more efficient ways to "cut to the chase" in order to be able to put anomaly detection to work in practical, real-world settings. Practical anomaly detection is more than just selecting the right algorithm and having the technical expertise to build the system—it also means finding solutions that take into account realistic limitations on resources, scheduling demands including time-to-value to make the projects cost effective, and correct understanding of business goals.

In this publication, we show you the underlying ideas of why anomaly detection works and what it's good for. We explore the idea of finding what is normal, deciding how to measure things that are far from normal and how far that must be to be considered an outlier (Chapters 2 and 3). We provide a new method to do this (t-digest) and look at how it can be applied in very simple systems (Chapter 3) and also in more complex systems (Chapters 4 and 5).

Throughout this report, we strongly recommend the use of adaptive, probabilistic models for predicting what is normal and how to contrast that to what is observed. One of our topics in Chapter 4 dabbles in deep learning with a time-series example, or at least dips its toe into the shallow end of that pool. Although this is an advanced concept, the execution of it in our example is surprisingly simple—no advanced math required.

Chapter 5 provides some very practical ways to model a system with sporadic events, such as website traffic or e-commerce purchases. In Chapter 6, we provide a practical illustration of many of the basic concepts in the form of detecting a phishing attack on a secure website. Let's see how all this works.

CHAPTER 2

The Shape of Anomaly Detection

The exciting thing about anomaly detection is the sense of discovery. You need a program that can spot what is unusual, so anomaly-detection models are on the lookout for the outliers. To get a sense of how this works, try a simple human-scale example, such as the one shown in Figure 2-1. Can you spot an outlier?

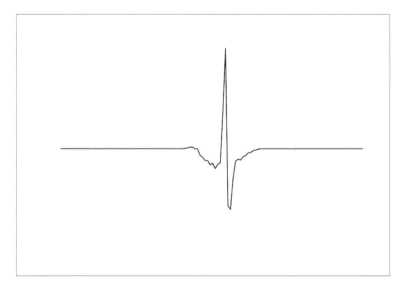

Figure 2-1. Can you spot an anomaly in this data?

Despite the fact that there is apparent noise in the data of the horizontal line shown in Figure 2-1, when you see data like this, it's fairly easy to see that the large spike appears to be an outlier. But is it?

What happens when you have a larger sample of data? Now your perception changes. What had appeared to be an anomaly turns out to be part of a regular and even familiar pattern: in this case, the regular frequency of a normally beating heart, recorded using an EKG, as shown in Figure 2-2.

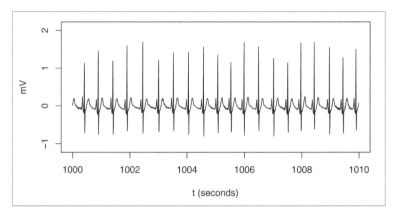

Figure 2-2. Normal heartbeat pattern recorded in an EKG. The spikes that had, in isolation, appeared to be anomalies relative to the horizontal curve are actually a regular and expected part of this normal pattern.

There's an important lesson here, even in this simple small-scale example:

> *Before you can spot an anomaly, you first have to figure out what "normal" is.*

Discovering " normal" is a little more complicated than it sounds, especially in a complex system. Often, to do this, you need a machine-learning model. To do this accurately, you also need a large enough sampling of data to get an accurate representation. Then you must find a way to analyze the data and mathematically define what forms a regular pattern in your training data.

Finding "Normal"

Let's think for a moment about the basic ideas that underlie anomaly detection, including the idea of discovering what is to be considered a normal pattern of behavior. One basic but powerful way to do this is to build a probabilistic model, an idea that we progressively develop here and in Chapters 3 through 6. A good way to think about this is in terms of mathematic symbols, but in case that's not your preference, consider the key ideas through this thought experiment.

Suppose you are studying birds in a particular location, and you observe, identify and count how many birds and of what species pass by a particular observation point over the course of days. An entirely made-up example of what these observations might look like is shown in Table 2-1.

Table 2-1. Bird watching provides a simple thought experiment to show how a probabilistic model works. Once a new species was observed, we watched for it on subsequent days. The synthetic data of this simplified example helps you think about how, based on the observations you've made, you could build a model to predict several things about what you expect to observe on Day x.

Species	Day 1	Day 2	Day 3	Day 4	Day 5	Day x
A	33	17	21	31	18	?
B	7	1	2	3	3	?
C	3	3	2	1	1	?
D	5	3	0	0	0	?
E	13	13	8	7	9	?
F	1	0	0	0	0	?
G	1	0	0	0	0	?
H	3	3	5	1	6	?
I	-	2	1	0	1	?
J	-	1	0	0	0	?
K	-	-	-	1	0	?
L	-	-	-	-	1	?
Next	-	-	-	-	-	?

Some species occur in fairly high numbers each day, and these species tend to be observed every day. Several species occur much less commonly. New species are seen almost every day, at least this early in the experiment. You can predict several things for a subsequent day (or short series of days):

- How many total birds you expect to see
- How many species you expect to see
- How many birds of each species will fly by

- How many new, previously unobserved, species will be seen

This prediction is nicely captured in the form of a probabilistic model. It assumes that all things (species) have at least some likelihood to occur, that some are more likely than others, and some are extremely rare (or not yet observed), and so the estimate of their likelihood will be a very small value. You can even predict how many new species you might expect on a given day, even if you cannot predict which species they will be. You can assign a probability for each event or type of event and thus describe in probabilistic terms what you estimate to be "normal."

If you enjoy math, read this description of a probabilistic model of "normal"...

For those of you who prefer a mathematical way to describe things, read on. For the rest of you, just skip this description and go to the next section.

Suppose that our best guess of the probability of some observation i from the set of all possible observation is π_i. The true underlying probability is p_i. Because our model is a probabilistic model, the values π_i are constrained by definition in the following way:

$$\pi_i \geq 0 \qquad p_i \geq 0$$

$$\sum_i \pi_i = 1 \quad \sum_i p_i = 1$$

What this means is that if we make π_i large for some i, then we have to make it smaller for some other i. Moreover, since the π_i have to all be non-negative, smaller means closer to zero but never less than zero. The very deep mathematical inference that we can draw here is that if *we make the average value of $-\log \pi_i$ as small as possible*, then we can prove that the estimated probabilities, π_i, will be as close as possible to the true underlying probabilities, p_i. In fact:

$$\max_{\pi} \sum_i p_i \log \pi_i = \sum_i p_i \log p_i$$

where the maximum is only achieved if $\pi_i = p_i$ for all i.

A rare event is expected to have a small value for π_i, and thus the value for $-\log \pi_i$ will all be a relatively large positive number. You might think that creates a problem, making the average $-\log \pi_i$ large when our best estimate of probabilities would need for it to be small. But remember that the average is computed by weighting things according to their probability, so that each rare thing will only have a small contribution.

Depending on the details of your data and what they represent, there are various ways to prepare data for use in such a model and a variety of appropriate algorithms from which to choose. We will describe several options in upcoming chapters.

Human Insight Helps

Discovering a normal pattern requires more than just a good machine-learning model. Part of the process of discovering normal involves human insight: you must interact with the modeling process to decide what makes sense in your own situation. The example of a single heartbeat shown in Figure 2-2 makes this point. In an abstract sense, the spike is anomalous as compared to the rest of the data. In our example, just collecting more data, such as what's shown in a full EKG, is more than enough to recognize that the spikes are a normal part of the heart function, but before seeing more data, an expert who knew it was an EKG being analyzed would also tell you that the spike was not an anomaly.

Our bird-watching thought experiment can also illustrate this point. Suppose you observe a brown pelican—is this to be expected? A domain expert would tell you yes, if you live near a coastal region of North America, or no if you live for instance in the inland state of North Dakota. Similarly, cedar waxwings are not seen for most of the year in California but sightings suddenly become relatively commonplace during a short period of migration. Of course the historical data would reveal these fluctuations, and this is just an analogy, but the point is that human insight from someone with domain knowledge is a valuable resource to put a probabilistic model into the proper context.

Continuing with our bird-watching thoughts, human experience might also inform you that some sequential events tend to be related. If you see one pelican fly by, it's reasonable to expect several more almost immediately because they often fly in a sort of squadron. But you would not expect a couple of hundred pelicans in rapid succession. This knowledge suggests to us not only that sequential measurements may not be entirely independent—an important concept—but also that models may require several levels of complexity to be really accurate predictions of real-world events.

So the first step in anomaly detection—using your model to discover what is normal—also requires human insight both to structure the model mathematically as well as to interpret what aspect of a pattern is of interest and whether or not it represents a reasonable view of a normal situation.

In building a machine-learning model for anomaly detection, you have to identify the best choice of data, figure out how to put it into a form acceptable to your algorithm and then acquire enough data for training your model. In other words you will use data initially to let the model discover patterns that you will then need to interpret in order to determine the baseline or normal situation. This may require a number of adjustments to the algorithm you use before you end up with something that makes sense. The more you know about the situation being investigated, the more easily and accurately you can decide when your model has achieved the first goal of anomaly detection by finding what is normal.

Finding Anomalies

A second level of human insight is needed once you've established what is normal and begin to look for what is anomalous. For our EKG example, anomalous behavior is not the fact that there are spikes but the observation that their frequency fluctuates during an episode of abnormal heart behavior, as seen in the data displayed in Figure 2-3.

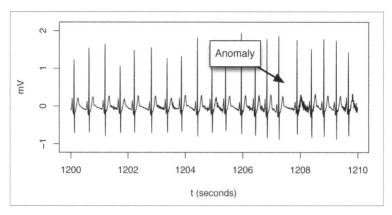

Figure 2-3. Anomalies in the frequency of the heartbeat show up as unevenly spaced spikes such as those between approximately 1206 and 1210 seconds in this EKG.

Figures 2-2 and 2-3 just illustrate the point that the basis for anomaly detection is to establish what is normal and then compare new events to that pattern or model. This two-step process can be done in a variety of ways from very simple models of fairly straightforward systems that use an assigned threshold to send alerts for potential anomalies (as described in Chapter 3) or more sophisticated models that are adaptive and can deal with complex or shifting situations (as explained in Chapters 4 through 6. In all of these cases, you are comparing observed behavior to what has been defined as normal.

Back to our bird-watching example: when the observations show either a big decrease in the overall number of common birds or the appearance of a large number of very rare birds, your model should flag the change as being anomalous.

Once again, if you like math, this description of anomalies is for you...

Thinking in terms of a probabilistic model, very rare, anomalous events will be assigned a much lower probability value than normal events during training. As a result, during an anomaly when we observe these rare events, the anomaly score will be large precisely because our estimate of their probability is very low.

Because an anomalous event has a lower probability value than those usually observed, the anomaly score, which is the negative log of the probability value, $-\log \pi_i$, will be larger, possibly much larger than usual. In other words, the anomaly score will be farther from the ideal maximum of zero. This increase suggests that our model's estimation of normal is less well matched to actual anomalous events—thus highlighting the occurrence of outliers.

Take-Home Lesson: Key Steps in Anomaly Detection

The overall message here is broadly applicable to different types of anomaly detection, regardless of the complexity of the system and the choice of algorithms that are used. These steps form a general guideline to goals when you are trying to build your own anomaly detector. Ask yourself these questions:

- What is normal?
- What will you measure to identify things that are "far" from normal?
- How far is "far", if something is to be considered anomalous?

A Simple Approach: Threshold Models

You must experiment to determine at what sensitivity you want your model to flag data as anomalous. If it is set too sensitively, random noise will get flagged, and with huge amounts of data, it will be essentially impossible to find anything useful beyond all the noise.

Even if you've adjusted the sensitivity to a coarser resolution such that your model is automatically flagging actual outliers, you still have a choice to make about the level of detection that is useful to you. There always are trade-offs between finding everything that is out of the ordinary and getting alarms at a rate for which you can handle making a response. These considerations, as well as a useful new way to set a good threshold, are the topic of Chapter 3.

Using *t*-Digest for Threshold Automation

The most common form of anomaly detector in use today is a manually-set threshold alarm to send an alert for possible anomalies. Input to such an alarm is a numerical measurement of some kind. The basic idea in this case is that whenever this measurement exceeds a threshold that you have set, possibly for a certain amount of time, an alarm is sounded.

This simple approach can work fairly well if the system being observed has a simple pattern of well-understood measurements, and the number of different kinds measurements is not enormous. But this approach can become quite difficult to carry out effectively if you have a large number of measurements with behaviors that you do not understand very well. As it turns out, that situation—a large number of measurements in a system that is either unpredictable or otherwise not well defined—is commonly encountered in real-world settings of interest. That's one reason we need some new ways to approach anomaly detection.

A good first step in improving these systems is to change the way that the threshold is set. Let's think about the goal for a threshold and how it can be optimized. Any particular value for a threshold will detect some fraction of the anomalies that you are trying to find, and if you have chosen the threshold well, that fraction of anomalies hopefully will be large. At the same time, this threshold most likely will sometimes trigger false alarms, in cases in which normal noise in the data is detected erroneously as being a true anomaly. Once again, if the system is built well and an appropriate threshold was chosen, the number of false alarms will be small. This trade-off between catching anomalies but trying to avoid too many false positives is what you are trying to optimize as you set the threshold.

If you are trying to detect anomalous positive deviations of the measurement you are collecting, then increasing the threshold will decrease the fraction of measurements that are false alarms (the false positive rate) but will also decrease the fraction of true anomalies we find (the true positive rate). Conversely, decreasing the threshold will have the opposite effect, finding more of the anomalies we are targeting but at the price of an increase in false positives. This decision is a trade-off between the two kinds of error: false positives and false negatives. The idea of these trade-offs is illustrated in Figure 3-1.

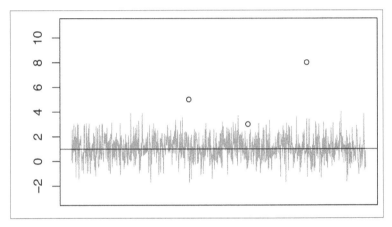

Figure 3-1. The idea of trade-offs in setting the threshold for alarm. The gray line is noisy but non-anomalous data. The black horizontal line shows the mean of the data—a crude model. The three circles are true anomalies. Where would you set a threshold to detect the anomalies without excessive false positives?

You could set a threshold to get a perfect record for catching anomalies, but then you've created a large and undesirable side effect of also getting a lot of what you don't want (false positives). This is a standard challenge in risk management that applies to much more than just monitoring systems—it also applies to many societal decisions.

The Philosophy Behind Setting the Threshold

The question you face is, "How many false positives are acceptable and what is the cost of possibly missing some real anomalies?" Roughly speaking, people fall into two broad groups in their goals for optimizing the threshold. These strategies are depicted in Figure 3-2. On one side are those for whom the major objective is to detect a very large fraction of anomalies because the penalty for missing any of them is great. An example might be a medical life-support device for which very sensitive detection of anomalies is important.

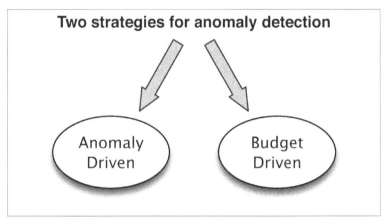

Figure 3-2. Goals for anomaly detection vary, and that in turn affects how you select a threshold. Anomaly-driven situations are those in which you have a required rate of detection and must estimate the number of false alarms in order to budget for that. Budget-driven anomaly detection occurs when you have a limited budget for response, and you must determine how many anomalies and false alarms you can handle within that budget, setting the threshold to match.

You could set the anomaly detection threshold very low in order to catch most or all anomalies, but this can result in a high rate of false positives. Dealing with false alarms also has a cost, however. You must have sufficient resources to respond to the alarms and determine whether or not they are false positives. Too many false alarms becomes a distraction, wastes time, and potentially overwhelms the human who needs to respond. This person could become habituated to the alarm, raising the danger that they will not respond appropriately to a true anomaly—it's a case of the danger of "crying wolf" too often. Even so, in a system with a high penalty for missed anomalies, you still have to choose the threshold to reduce the rate of missed anomalies to the required level. Given that threshold, you then calculate what you must budget in time and expense to handle anomalies and the many false positives you are likely to have.

In contrast is the budget-driven philosophy in which you have to work with a fixed budget for dealing with all alarms. In this case, your budget drives your choice of threshold, even if it means missing some true anomalies. For a whimsical example, consider measurements in a chocolate candy factory. The measurement in question might be the input and output amount of chocolate, or how many chocolate nuggets are dropped in each bag, or the ratio of chocolate and peanuts for each piece of candy. The anomalies you would like to detect might include temperature fluctuations of the melted chocolate, problems with viscosity, or errors in the swing of a mechanical arm that extrudes a stream of chocolate. While it might seem heartbreaking to your loyal customers to end up with a charred taste because the system overheated the chocolate one day, it's not life-threatening. In this case, you are likely to be driven by a trade-off of the cost of dealing with alarms to alert you to fluctuations versus the potential threat to producing a batch of candy that will disappoint your customers.

Ideally, in general, you want to have as high a true positive rate as you can, but you also have a maximum number of false positives that you can afford to deal with. You must therefore choose your threshold to control the total alarms in a given time period. Theoretically, you should be able to set this threshold by examining the distribution of the measurement under normal conditions and picking a value of the threshold to give the desired rate of alarms. This assumption is an especially good fit for the budget-driven situations.

As an example, suppose that we have a measurement that is made once per second, and we are willing to investigate three false positives per month. We will have about 3 million measurements per month, so we can accept about one false positive per million measurements. In that case, the threshold should be set to roughly the 99.9999th percentile. That action may sound easy, but incrementally calculating an extreme quantile accurately with limited memory can be difficult, especially if you need to do this for a large number of related situations. In the next section, we will describe how to use a new algorithm, t-digest, to estimate extreme quantiles on large data sets in an online fashion.

Another consideration is that, in practice, successive measurements are often highly correlated. (Remember the squadron of pelicans we mentioned in the analogy in Chapter 2?) When measurements exhibit such correlations, we may want to consider short batches of inputs instead of individual points when setting the threshold. In the example above with one measurement per second, we might actually only have the equivalent of one independent measurement every 5 minutes and thus would consider 5-minute batches instead of individual points. In that case, to get the desired 3 alarms per month, we want to allow one 5-minute batch or about 300 measurements above the threshold per million measurements, and the threshold should be set to the 99.97th percentile. The measurements that exceed the threshold will occur in bunches due to correlation, and the total number of alerts we have to respond to will be much less than the number of measurements above the threshold.

In either case, percentiles are a very natural scale for talking about the threshold setting. Translating a percentile into a threshold can be tricky with limited memory and time, however. That's where t-digest can help.

Using t-Digest for Accurate Calculation of Extreme Quantiles

The data structure known as t-digest was developed by one of the authors, Ted Dunning, as a way to accurately estimate extreme quantiles for very large data sets with limited memory use. This capability makes t-digest particularly useful for selecting a good threshold for anomaly detection. The t-digest algorithm is available in Apache Mahout as part of the Mahout math library. It's also available as open source at *https://github.com/tdunning/t-digest* and has been published to Maven Central. The t-digest algorithm has been picked up by several other projects, including Elasticsearch and stream-lib.

One of the advantages of t-digest is **accuracy**, especially for extreme quantiles; another is making the problem **less cumbersome** by requiring limited amounts of memory. Instead of having to sort a large number of samples to estimate a quantile of interest, an incoming signal can be analyzed in an online fashion using a t-digest to find the threshold corresponding to any quantile. This process is shown in Figure 3-3. The threshold is selected in terms of which percentile of the distribution of the incoming signal is desired. In this case, a threshold of 99.97% has been selected. To alert us of negative deviations, the sign of the comparison would be reversed, and a low percentile would be selected instead of a high one.

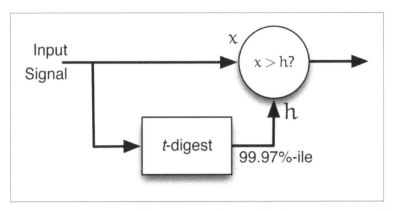

Figure 3-3. Using the t-digest to set a threshold. The incoming signal (x) is routed to the t-digest to estimate the threshold (h) as a quantile. New incoming data is compared to this threshold.

Issues with Simple Thresholds

The basic idea behind any anomaly detector is that we are building a model of the input to the detector—our estimation of "normal"—looking for deviations from that model. The model for the threshold-based anomaly detector is based on an assumption that the incoming signal has a nearly stationary and simple distribution so that a particular percentile will always be at a particular point. If this assumption doesn't hold, and often it does not, then the threshold as computed by the t-digest will result in the rate of true and false positives to vary as the distribution of the signal changes. Figure 3-4 shows an example of a signal that exhibits this problem.

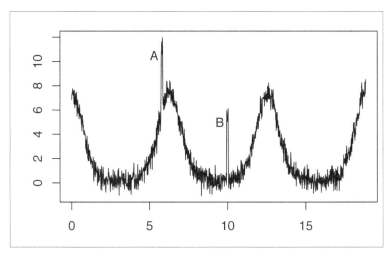

Figure 3-4. A non-stationary distribution can make it hard to see some anomalies using a simple threshold.

With any kind of simple threshold detector, the anomaly at A in Figure 3-4 will be detected easily, but the anomaly at B will not, even though they are both much larger than the noise level.

Clearly, we need a more nuanced and adaptive kind of model to handle this sort of problem. We will explore how to do this in the next chapter.

CHAPTER 4

More Complex, Adaptive Models

As we saw in the previous chapter, it is relatively easy to build the very simplest anomaly detector that looks for deviations from an ideal value. Tools like the *t*-digest can help by analyzing historical data to accurately find a good threshold. Statistically, such a system is building a *model* of the input data that describes the data as a constant value with some additive noise. For a system like most of the ones we have seen so far, the model is nearly trivial, but it is a model nonetheless.

But what about the more complicated situations, such as the one shown at the end of the last chapter in Figure 3-3? Systems that are not stationary or that have complicated patterns even when they are roughly periodic require something more than a simple threshold detector. And what happens when conditions change?

What is needed is an adaptive machine-learning model for anomaly detection. In Chapter 2 we discussed the idea of a probabilistic model that is trained using histories of past events to estimate their likelihood of occurrence as a way to describe what is normal. This type of model is adaptive: as small fluctuations occur in the majority of events, our model can adjust its view of "normal" accordingly. In other words, it adapts to reasonable variations. Back to our bird-watching analogy, if our bird detector is looking for unusual species ("accidentals" in bird-watching jargon) or significant and possibly catastrophic changes in the population of normal species, we might want our model to be able to adjust to small changes in the local population that respond to slight shifts in weather conditions, availability of seeds and water, or excessive activity of the neighbor's cat. We want our model to be adaptive.

Conceptually, it is relatively easy to imagine extending the constant threshold model of Chapter 3 by allowing the mean value to vary and then set all thresholds relative to that mean value. Statistically speaking, what we are doing is describing our input as a time-varying base value combined with additive noise that has constant distribution and zero mean. By building a model of exactly how we expect that base value to vary, we can build an anomaly detector that produces an alert whenever the input behaves sufficiently differently from what is expected.

Let's take a look at the EKG signal that we talked about in Chapter 2 of this report. The pulses in the EKG that record the heartbeats of the patient being measured are each highly similar to one another. In fact, substantial changes in the shape of the waveforms in the EKG often indicate either some sort of physiological problem or equipment malfunction. So the problem of anomaly detection in an EKG can be viewed as the problem of how to build a model of what heartbeats *should* look like, and then how to compare the observed heartbeats to this ideal model. If the model is a good one—in other words a good estimate of normal heart behavior—then a measurement of error for observed behavior relative to this ideal model will highlight anomalous behavior. *If the magnitude of the error stands out*, it may be a flag that highlights irregular heartbeats or a failure in the monitor. This approach can work to find anomalies in a variety of situations, not just for an EKG.

To understand this mathematically (just stay with us), think back to Chapter 2, in which we stated that anomaly detection involves modeling what is normal, looking for events that lie far from normal, and having to decide how to determine that. In the type of example described in this current chapter, we have a continuous measurement, and at any point in time, we have a single value. The probabilistic model for "normal" in this situation involves a sum of a base value plus random noise. We can estimate the base value using our model, and subtracting this from our observational input data leaves the random noise, which is our **reconstruction error**. According to our model, the error noise has an average value of zero and stationary distribution. When the remaining noise is large, we have an anomaly, and t-digest can decide what we should consider a large value of noise to be.

Windows and Clusters

We still have the challenge of finding an approachable, practical way to model normal for a very complicated curve such as the EKG. To do this, we are going to turn to a type of machine learning known as deep learning, at least in an introductory way. Here's how.

Deep learning involves letting a system learn in several layers, in order to deal with large and complicated problems in approachable steps. With a nod toward this approach, we've found a simple way to do this for curves such as the EKG that have repeated components separated in time rather than superposed. We take advantage of the repetitive and separated nature of an EKG curve in order to accurately model its complicated shape.

Figure 4-1 shows an expanded view of two heartbeats from an EKG signal. Each heartbeat consists of several phases or pulses that correspond to electrical activity in the heart. The first part of the heartbeat is the P wave, followed by the QRS complex, or group of pulses, and then the T wave. The recording shown here was made with a portable recording device and doesn't show all of the detail in the QRS complex, nor is the U wave visible just after the T wave. The thing to notice is that each wave is strikingly similar from heartbeat to heartbeat. That heart is beating in a normal pattern.

To build a model that uses this similarity, we use a mathematical trick called *windowing*. It's a way of dealing with the regular but complex patterns when you need to build a model that can accurately predict them. This method involves extracting short sequences of the original signal in such a way that that the short sequences can be added back together to re-create the original signal.

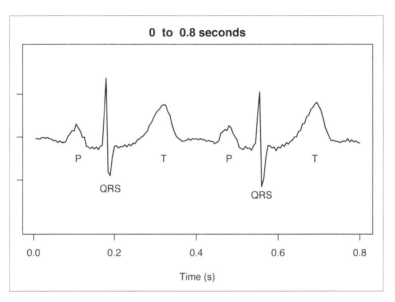

Figure 4-1. An EKG signal is comprised of components that are complex but highly repetitive.

The first step of our analysis is to do windowing to break up the larger pattern into small components. Figure 4-2 shows how the EKG for these two heartbeats are broken up into a sequence of nine overlapping short signals. As you can see, several of these signals are similar to each other. This similarity can be exploited to build a heartbeat model by aligning and clustering all of the short signals observed in a long recording. In this example, the clustering was done using a ball k-means algorithm from the Apache Mahout library. We chose this algorithm because our sample data here is not huge, so we could do this as an in-memory operation. With larger data sets, we might have done the clustering with a different algorithm, such as streaming k-means, also from Mahout.

The clustering operation essentially builds a catalog of these shapes so that the original signal can be encoded by simply recording which shape from the catalog is used in each time window, along with a scaling factor for each shape.

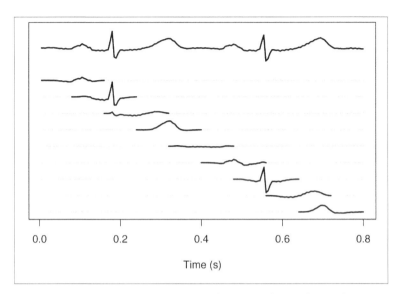

Figure 4-2. Windowing decomposes the original signal into short segments that can be added together to reconstruct the original signal.

By looking at a long time series of data from an EKG, you can construct a *dictionary of component shapes* that are typical for normal heart behavior. Figure 4-3 shows a selection of 64 out of 400 shapes from a dictionary constructed based on several hours of a real EKG recording. These shapes clearly show some of the distinctive patterns found in EKG recordings.

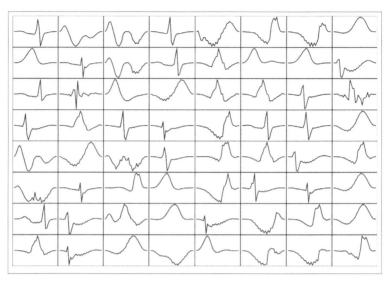

Figure 4-3. Dictionary of component shapes. Clustering finds the most commonly used signal shapes for reconstructing a representation of normal heartbeats.

Matches with the Windowed Reconstruction: Normal Function

Now let's see what happens when this technique is applied to a new EKG signal. Remember, the goal here is to build a model of an observed signal, compare it to the ideal model, and note the level of error between the two. We assume that the shapes used as components (the dictionary of shapes shown in Figure 4-3) are accurate depictions of a normal signal. Given that, a low level of errors in the comparison between the re-constructed signal and the ideal suggests that the observed signal is close to normal. In contrast, a large error points to a mismatch. *This is not a test of the reconstruction method but rather a test of the observed signal.* A mismatch indicates an abnormal signal, and thus an anomaly in heart function.

Figure 4-4 shows a reconstruction of an EKG signal. The top trace is the original signal, the middle one is the reconstructed signal, and the bottom trace shows the difference between the first two. This last signal shows how well the reconstruction encodes the original signal and is called the *reconstruction error*.

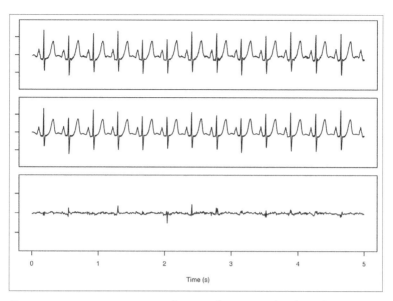

Figure 4-4. Reconstruction of normal pattern for heartbeats using windowing and clustering. The reconstruction error (bottom trace) for an EKG signal (top trace) is computed by subtracting the reconstructed signal (middle trace) from the original. Notice that the reconstruction error (bottom trace) is small and relatively uniform.

As long as the original signal looks very much like the signals that were used to create the shape dictionary, the reconstruction will be very good, and the reconstruction error will be small. The dictionary is thus a model of what EKG signals can look like, and the reconstruction error represents the degree to which the signal being reconstructed looks like a heartbeat. A large reconstruction error occurs when the input does not look much like a heartbeat (or, in other words, is anomalous).

Note in Figure 4-4 how the reconstruction error has a fixed baseline. This fact suggests that we can apply a thresholding anomaly detector as described in Chapter 3 to the reconstruction error to get a complete anomaly detector. Figure 4-5 shows a block diagram of an anomaly detector built based on this idea.

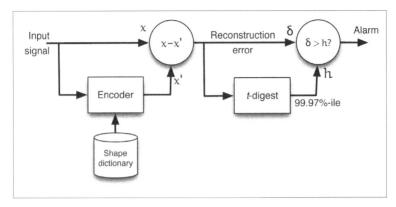

Figure 4-5. Signal reconstruction error from an auto-encoder can be used to find anomalies in a complex signal. Input signal x is analyzed using an encoder, which reconstructs x using a model in the form of a shape dictionary to produce a reconstructed signal x'. The difference, x-x', is the reconstruction error δ. Comparing δ to a threshold h gives us an alarm signal when the encoder cannot reconstruct x accurately as indicated by a large reconstruction error δ.

Essentially what is happening here is that the encoder can only reproduce very specific kinds of signals. The encoder is used to reduce the complex input signal to a reconstruction error, which is large whenever the input isn't the kind of signal the encoder can handle. This reconstruction error is just the sort of stationary signal that is appropriate for use with the methods described in Chapter 3, and so we can use the *t*-digest on the reconstruction error to look for anomalies.

Mismatches with the Windowed Reconstruction: Anomalous Function

That this approach can find interesting anomalies is shown in Figure 4-6, where you can see a spike in the reconstruction error just after 101 seconds. It is clear that the input signal (top trace) is not faithfully rendered by the reconstruction, but at this scale, it is hard to see exactly why.

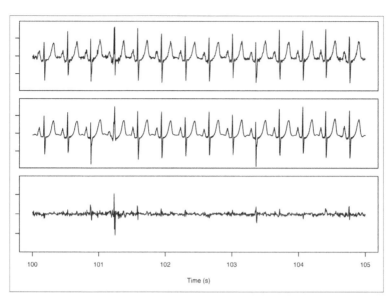

Figure 4-6. Reconstruction for a heart signal displaying anomalous behavior. Top trace is the original EKG signal. The bottom trace shows the reconstruction error that is computed by subtracting the reconstructed signal (middle trace) from the original. Notice the spike in the error at just past 101 seconds. That error spike indicates that the reconstruction shown in the middle panel was unable to reproduce that section of the original signal shown at the top.

If you expand the time scale, however, it is easy to see what is happening. Figure 4-7 shows that at about 101.25 seconds, the QRS complex in the heartbeat is actually a double pulse. This double pulse is very different from anything that appears in a recording of a normal heartbeat, and that means that there isn't a shape in the dictionary that can be used to reconstruct this signal.

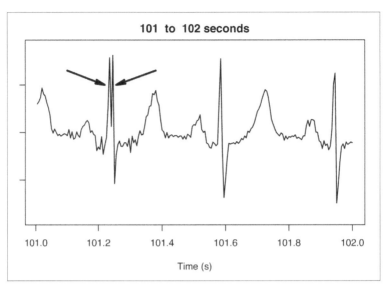

Figure 4-7. Expanded view of the anomalous heartbeat. The anomaly (indicated by arrows) was detected by finding an unusually large reconstruction error.

This kind of anomaly detector can't say what the anomaly is. All it can do is tell us that something unusual has happened. Expert human judgment is required for the interpretation of the physiological meaning of this anomaly, but having a system that can draw attention to where human judgment should best be applied helps if only by avoiding fatigue.

Other systems can make use of this general model-based signal reconstruction technique. The signal doesn't have to be as perfectly periodic for this to work, and it can involve multidimensional inputs instead of just a single signal. The key is that there is a model that can encode the input very concisely. You can find the code and data used in this example on GitHub (*https://github.com/tdunning/anomaly-detection*).

A Powerful But Simple Technique

Note that the model used here to encode the EKG signal is fairly simple. The technique used to produce this model gives surprisingly good results given its low level of complexity. It can be used to analyze signals in a variety of situations including sound, vibration, or flow, such as what might be encountered in manufacturing or other industrial settings. Not all signals can be accurately analyzed with a model as simple as the one used here, particularly if the fundamental patterns are superposed as opposed to separated, as with the EKG. Such superposed signals may require a more elaborate model. Even the EKG signal requires a fancier model if we want to not only see the shape of the individual heartbeats but also features such as irregular heartbeats. One approach for building a more elaborate model is to use deep learning to build a reconstruction model that understands a waveform on both short and long time scales. The model shown here can be extended to a form of deep learning by recursively clustering the groups of cluster weights derived by the model described here.

Regardless, however, of the details of the model itself, the architecture shown here will still work for inputs roughly like this one or even inputs that consist of many related measurements.

The EKG model we discussed was an example of a system with a continuous signal having a single value at any point in time. A reconstruction-model approach can also be used for a different type of system, one with multiple measurements being made at a single point in time. An example of a multidimensional system like this is a community water supply system. With the increasing use of sensors in such systems that report many different system parameters, you might encounter thousands of measurements for a single point in time. These measurements could include flow or pressure at multiple locations in the system, or depth measurements for reservoirs. Although this type of system has a huge number of data points at any single time stamp, it does not exhibit the complex dynamics of the heartbeat/EKG example. To make a probabilistic model of such a multidimensional water system, you might use a fairly sophisticated approach such as neural nets or a physics-based model, but for anomaly detection, you can still use a reconstruction error–based technique.

Looking Toward Modeling More Problematic Inputs

Where this approach really begins to break down a bit is with inputs that are not based on a measurement of a value such as voltage, pressure, or flow. A good example of such a problematic input can be found in the log files from a website. In that case, the input consists of events that have a time of occurrence and some kind of label. Even though the methods described in this chapter can't be applied verbatim, the basic idea of a probabilistic model is still the key to good anomaly detection. The use of an adaptive, probabilistic model for e-commerce log files is the topic of the next chapter.

CHAPTER 5

Anomalies in Sporadic Events

The input signals in the examples discussed in previous chapters have all been values sampled at uniform intervals. Such signals make it easy to talk about a reconstructed value computed by a model and the difference between that value and the original input the reconstruction error.

In practice, however, there are other forms of data that are important to process for anomaly detection. One important class of such data is known as an event stream and is usually derived from log files of one sort or another. A key characteristic of these log files is that they record events that occur at irregular intervals.

It is also fairly common for these events to be associated with a symbolic value such as your IP address and the URL of a web page you visit if page views are the input of interest. Another input might be stock trades, for which the symbolic values could include the stock sign and be combined with the trades, price, and number of shares. Other examples of this type of input are e-commerce purchases or Internet packets. In each of these cases, we want to be able to detect anomalous activity in these event streams, such as changes in the rate or geolocation of web traffic, or perhaps the number of stock trades in particular time periods in stock markets. Sometimes the anomaly of interest is the absence of activity during a particular time interval, and that can be a challenge for anomaly detection models to handle.

Because these events occur at irregular times and because they have symbolic values rather than numerical values, it is hard to imagine how to use the techniques from the previous chapters to find anomalies in event streams. As we will see, however, there are fundamental unifying principles that let us extend the previous methods to handle event streams.

Counts Don't Work Well

You might think that doing anomaly detection on event streams is as easy as simply counting how many events occur in successive fixed-length time intervals and then considering that count as a measurement to be used with the approaches described earlier in this report. There are, however, several problems with this count-based approach.

The first problem occurs because counts have inherent variation due to statistical fluctuations. This variation can make it hard to detect any small or moderate changes in system behavior without long accumulation periods. In order to detect outages reliably, we need the average counts in each period to be fairly large. We can fix this problem by making the counting interval longer to accumulate sufficient counts in each interval.

But correcting this first problem creates a second problem. Waiting long enough to accumulate a large count makes it essentially impossible to detect anomalies quickly unless the event rate is really large. These ideas are illustrated in Figure 5-1.

Look at the left panel in Figure 5-1, which shows frequent sampling with a short time interval. Although the rate of events being counted increases by 20% for intervals from about half to three-quarters through the 200-minute observation period, this fluctuation is hard to recognize buried in the large statistical variation inherent in small counts.

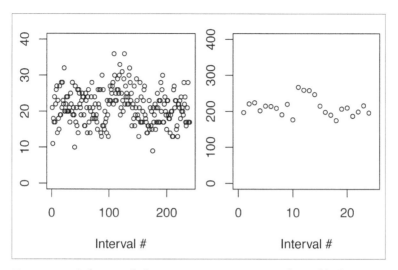

Figure 5-1. Substantial changes in rate are not easily visible for count data with relatively low rate and short counting intervals. Left and right panels show the same data sampled over a total of 200 minutes. Each data point in the left panel shows the sum of counts for that one-minute interval. In the right panel, the sampling interval was increased to 10 minutes, so there are fewer total intervals, and the count for each one is 10 times larger. Notice that the fluctuation seen at about half to three quarters of the way through the observation period is much easier to see in the right panel with its longer counting intervals.

In the righthand panel, in contrast, the shift is distinctly visible, but only at the cost of increasing the collection periods by a factor of 10. While this makes the change visible, it also increases the time required to detect any change, even a catastrophic one, and thus limits your ability to respond quickly. In short, this overall situation presents a challenging signal-to-noise problem. That's why counts per time interval is not a good measurement to use when modeling systems that have sporadic events.

In some systems, events arrive at such a high rate that you can have both large counts and short intervals. It's acceptable to use counts as the measure for modeling in these high-rate systems, and that makes it easy to process them using methods described in our previous chapters. Many systems aren't like this, however, and summarizing the event arrival data as counts leads to an unacceptable choice between detecting small changes and responding quickly to large changes.

The solution to this problem is to look at an event stream as it is, as events with arrival times, rather than trying to convert it into periodic counts.

Arrival Times Are the Key

In sporadic event systems, the varying time between events does present a challenge, but the situation improves if you use arrival time rather than counts as what you measure. Before, we asked, "What is the count for a fixed-time interval?" Now we can turn that around and ask, "What is the time interval for a fixed count?"

Even though we've changed which measurement we will use for our model, the questions we want to ask about our sporadic event system are really the same. What is the rate of events? Is a new pattern showing up? Did everything stop?

Let's consider the problem of how to know if our event stream has stopped—in other words, how to tell the difference between irregular time intervals (normal) and the cessation of events (anomaly). The key observation when things cease is that the time since the last event increases without bounds. In normal circumstances, the time since the last event may be irregular, but it is not unbounded. We can approach this problem by setting an alarm based on some time period beyond what is reasonable to expect for the next event. If an event does occur before the alarm, we simply reset the alarm into the future. Using the style of rolling alarms, we still must decide what should be our reference point for the alarms and how best to estimate when the next event is expected so that we know when to begin to worry if nothing shows up. Figure 5-2 gives you a simple framework to think about a couple of choices for one of those issues: how to chose a useful reference point.

If you want to have the quickest ability to respond to a problem, your reference point should be based on the time of the last event. This approach is good if we are trying to spot a complete cessation, but normal variation in the time between events (the noise in our measurement) makes it hard to spot a less-than-catastrophic change in rate of events using the last event as our reference.

To detect a change in rate, you need to smooth out the noise by looking at more events as your reference when setting the alarm. You do this by choosing a previous event that was several events ago (*nth* event ago) as the reference. You are still setting an alarm based on watching for the presence or absence of the next event, but your estimate for it is across more events and therefore has a larger signal-to-noise ratio. If you want to detect the rate increasing, you set a minimum time; for a decrease in rate, you set a maximum time.

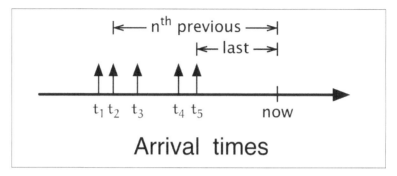

Figure 5-2. The key parameter to model sporadic events is the arrival time. You can consider the time to the last event for quickest response or to some previous event that you choose for the most accuracy, which is helpful in systems with fairly low rate of events.

Keep in mind that there are two parts of systems using anomaly detection. One is the alert system, such as a dashboard or other possibly pre-existing application to set alerts and send alarms. The other is a measurement system that you are building, your program to calculate normal rate and record when each event arrives. You might arrange to have rolling alarms driven by having the measurement system in charge: it sets the time interval for alarms and then measures when a new arrival occurs in order to reset each alarm. Or you could design a system with the alert center in charge: periodically it generates a query to ask how long it was to a reference event (last or earlier) and is that OK? Either way, the choice between quickest response time using last event as a reference or best accuracy using an *nth* event still applies.

All of this discussion about deadlines for the next event pre-supposes that we know what the rate should be. We must have a way to estimate that rate, usually based on historic files. How we do that differs with different sporadic event systems. Some are fairly challenging to estimate, and in some cases we can use a clever simplification as shown in a later section.

And Now with the Math…

The way that we searched for anomalies in the previous chapters was to build a model to reconstruct a signal and then look at the reconstruction error. Large errors signaled the presence of anomalies. Mathematically speaking, that method is very similar to constructing a model composed of two parts: the reconstruction model and an error process. Commonly, this error process is assumed to be distributed according to the normal distribution. With that assumption, the log of the probability of the reconstruction is very nearly proportional to the square of the reconstruction error.

For independent events that occur at random times, squared error doesn't work, and it is common to describe the distribution of these events in terms of a variable rate Poisson process. A Poisson process describes events that occur independently in time at a fixed rate. This reasoning can be extended to allow the rate to vary. The useful part about this kind of model for anomaly detection is that the log of the probability of the time between events is proportional to the time between events multiplied by the rate. If we have a model for the rate itself, then the time between events can serve just as the reconstruction error did in previous chapters. We can use it to identify when the rate predicted by our model varies significantly from the actual observed rate and thus flag an anomaly.

Figure 5-3 shows an example of how such a model might be built for an event source that exhibits predictable variation in traffic. Remember that in our approach, we are asking the question, "What is the time interval for a fixed count?". In our anomaly detection model, the constant is the interval from now back to a certain number of previous events that we designate, and our variable is the length of time that interval takes. We use the parameter n to designate which previous event bounds our interval. For example, if $n=1$, the interval used is the time since the most recent event. When we set $n>1$, we get the time since the nth earlier event. When we use $n=1$, we get the fastest response. With $n>1$, we can see smaller rate changes, but there is a bit more delay before the change can be seen.

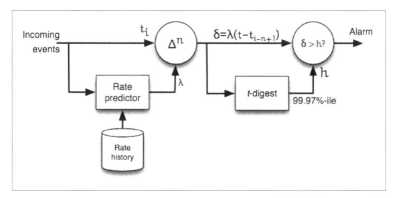

Figure 5-3. Event arrival time of the most recent event (t_i) is used by the rate predictor to update the rate history and to compute an estimate of current event rate (λ). This event rate is multiplied by the time from now (at time t) back to the nth most recent event to compute the analog of the reconstruction error (δ). An alarm is triggered when δ exceeds the threshold (h). Note that when n=1, the expression ($t - t_i - n + 1$) becomes $t - t_i$, the time to the most recent event.

The key to making an anomaly detector of this sort work well is to build a good rate predictor. Exactly how that is done depends very much on the system you are analyzing. The next section shows how you can do this for a website.

Event Rate in a Worked Example: Website Traffic Prediction

Here's a handy practical machine learning method that makes it easy to predict events and discover anomalies for website traffic as opposed to other types of sporadic event systems. A consumer-facing website typically has traffic patterns that repeat each day and each week, especially if the majority of the audience is located within one or a few time zones. Traffic goes up when a majority of the audience for the site is awake and browsing and goes down when they are asleep. This roughly repeated variation with time is called *seasonality* by econometricians, even if the variation occurs on a daily or weekly basis rather than an annual basis. Almost all websites show this sort of seasonality pattern. The exact nature of the traffic patterns varies, however. Some sites have more traffic on weekends and some have more traffic during the week. In any case, the pattern itself is often amazingly stable and thus can be exploited in building a traffic-rate predictor. As we saw before, an event rate is the key element in an event anomaly detector; once that is working, it is relatively easy to integrate the traffic model into the system shown in Figure 5-3.

This section shows how you can exploit daily and weekly seasonality to get traffic-rate prediction accurate enough for good anomaly detection. The example here deals with Wikipedia traffic logs, but the patterns for e-commerce sites are very similar. The model here uses combinations of traffic rates from prior hours to model the current traffic rate. Figure 5-4 shows the hourly number of visits to the English language main page for Wikipedia for the month of November 2008. The graph shows hourly visits as well as hourly visits delayed by exactly a week so that we can look at how closely the traffic pattern repeats week to week. This particular month starts on a weekend at A. One week later at B, we see that the weekend pattern is almost exactly repeated. In fact, it is a bit hard to see the delayed graph. During the next week, the match is a little bit less precise. At C there is an anomaly in the recorded traffic, probably due to a data-handling bug rather than a real traffic spike. During the week of the 17th, we see traffic continue at a lower level than the previous week, which makes sense because the end of the month of November is when the major US holiday Thanksgiving occurs and some people are probably leaving work early. You can see the holiday itself at D, as two weekdays have traffic patterns more like a Saturday than a Thursday and Friday. If you look closely, you can even see when people start eating Thanksgiving day dinner (or start to watch the football game) on November 28th.

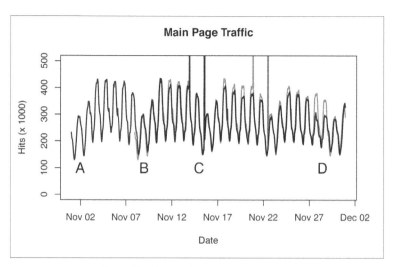

Figure 5-4. Hourly traffic for Wikipedia main page for the month of November, 2008. The dark line is the actual traffic. The light gray line is the traffic delayed by a week.

What this shows us is that simply using the traffic rate from exactly one week ago can give a remarkably precise estimate of what current traffic levels should be, but holidays can degrade accuracy. If you want a more accurate estimate, you may want to build a real regression model with additional predictor variables like lagged values of hourly data. It is typically easiest to regress on the log of traffic rather than try to predict the exact value of current traffic since this allows the regression to be done using linear methods.

With one or another of these techniques, it is usually possible to build a traffic model for a high-traffic website that is accurate to within about 5% of the actual traffic. Sometimes the simple week-delayed model suffices, and sometimes you may require the slightly fancier kind of regression model, but one or the other should suffice. For websites with lower traffic levels, it is harder to build such an accurate model, but the same techniques achieve sufficient accuracy to build a useful traffic anomaly monitor.

Extreme Seasonality Effects

The simple week-delay model is not sufficient during periods of extreme variation related to seasonality, such as major holidays. To show this with our Wikipedia example, we asked what happens for page views related to a seasonal topic. Figure 5-5 shows the hourly traffic for the Wikipedia page about Christmas for the last 45 days of 2008. The limitations of the simple week-delay model are very clear.

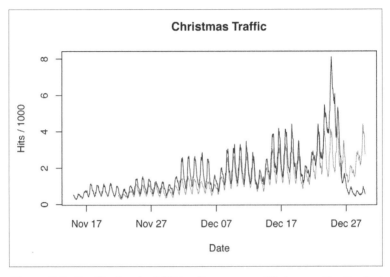

Figure 5-5. Traffic for the Wikipedia page on Christmas for the last part of 2008. The dark line is the actual traffic. One week delayed traffic is in gray.

During the last week of November, traffic predictions are still reasonably good, but the first week in December shows a dramatic increase in traffic with the simple delay model underestimating peak traffic by nearly 2:1. Interestingly, the second and third weeks of December have better prediction. During the week of Christmas itself, the delay model falls apart again. The week after Christmas, the anomaly detector would probably decide that Christmas had "broken" since traffic is less than 25% of what would be predicted.

For situations such as this where substantial variations occur on top of seasonality, we need to increase the complexity of our model. In this example, the approach we chose was to build a standard linear model in R using the glm function. We used logs of rates in our model because it is more natural to think about relative changes in rate rather than absolute changes. We set up our model to find the linear relationship between predictors (lagged log of average rates in the training data) and target variable (the log of current rate in the training data). We built a training dataset with these target rates and predictors, as illustrated in Figure 5-6.

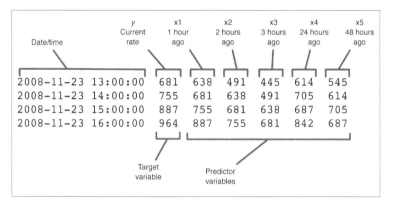

Figure 5-6. Illustration of part of the training data for our traffic model. The current rate for each hour is the target variable, and rates from 1, 2, 3, 24 and 48 hours earlier are the predictor variables. Note how the value 681 appears as current and delayed values on successive lines.

Using R, we estimated a formula that connects together the different predictors and gives us an estimate of current rate:

$$\log y = a_1 \log x_1 + a_2 \log x_2 + a_3 \log x_3 + a_4 \log x_4 + a_5 \log x_5$$

where a, a_1, a_2, a_3, a_4, and a_5 are the regression coefficients.

Figure 5-7 shows the results of our linear model that predicts traffic based on lagged data to get an estimate. The model was trained on the 600 hours of traffic from November 22 until December 17 and then applied to traffic after that period.

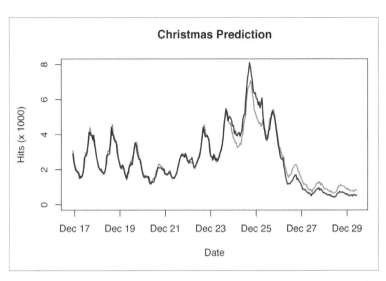

Figure 5-7. Traffic prediction in the face of extreme change in traffic levels. The actual traffic is in black, and the predicted traffic is in gray. Predictions are fairly accurate well into the extreme high-traffic period and even after the post-Christmas collapse.

This more elaborate model produces very good predictions until the night before Christmas and then under-predicts traffic by about 25% on Christmas day. As traffic collapses the day after Christmas, the model over-predicts traffic, which could lead to some malfunctioning of the anomaly detector, but within a week, accuracy returns to prior levels.

Even with this degradation in accuracy, if you decrease the amount of history that the quantile estimator is allowed, the anomaly detector functions well through the holiday season in spite of radical shifts in traffic patterns. Note that one-year delayed data is not likely to help as much because annual traffic patterns change due to how most holidays fall on different days of the week each year.

The point here is that even during periods where traffic patterns change radically, fairly straightforward traffic rate models can be sufficiently accurate to allow event-rate anomaly detectors to be built using simple techniques. It may be that the inclusion of annual data would improve these models a bit, but the models shown here provide high enough accuracy to make that unnecessary.

CHAPTER 6

No Phishing Allowed!

One of the most important uses for anomaly detection is to identify potentially fraudulent behavior and thus reduce risk of loss and improve security. The nefarious behaviors to be found could be credit card fraud, identity theft, or phishing attacks on a secure website such as an online banking site. It's not only challenging to think of how to create an effective model and alert system—it's also a challenge to stay one step (or even two) ahead of the fraudsters. As you find ways to foil their attacks, they keep looking for new ways to commit theft. In this situation, agility, cost-effective and practical approaches, and innovation are all required.

Let's take a look at a method that lets a machine-learning model quickly identify a hypothetical phishing attack on a bank site and flag it as suspicious. This example will extend the concepts of a probabilistic model that we have developed in previous chapters to situations that involve *sequences* of events.

The Phishing Attack

The attack is based on luring bank customers to a fake website in order to capture their private login details. The plan also includes having the customer unknowingly type in the CAPTCHA security code for the fraudsters that their fraud-bot script would not be able to do by itself without human help. A description of how the fraud might be attempted is given here and summarized in Figure 6-1.

Step 1

A huge number of customers receive an automated email that appears to be from the bank. The email presents some enticing reason that the customer would want to click the link provided that supposedly goes to the URL of the bank. A lot of people ignore such messages, but some customers inevitably will believe the email is genuine and click the link. What happens next?

Step 2

When an unsuspecting customer clicks the link, they reach what looks very much like the familiar website of their own bank. Even the images on the site are identical. The customer obligingly types in their login ID and password and successfully works out the always-hard-to-read CAPTCHA code word and types that in as well.

Step 3

Now two things happen: the customer is redirected to a page with an "oops" message screen indicating that they made an error typing in their login details or CAPTCHA and asking them to click to log in again. They do so. Meanwhile, the fraud-bot script has been busily stealing the customer's login information that was originally typed into the fake-bank website.

Step 4

On their second attempt, the customer successfully logs into the real bank site. They see that their funds are in place and feel secure. But…

Step 5

…the fraud bot can use the captured login details to reach the customer's account and merrily withdraw all the money—a big phish indeed.

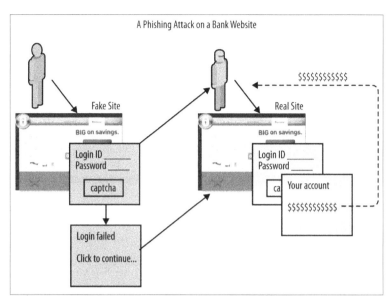

Figure 6-1. The steps in a phishing attack on an online banking site. An email is used to lure a customer to the fake site that looks like an online bank. When the customer attempts to log in, the fraud bot captures the information and uses it to log in to the real site to transfer out the funds. The user is meanwhile directed to the real login page, where they can log in, unaware that their account has been compromised.

How can this fraud attack be detected quickly?

The No-Phishing-Allowed Anomaly Detector

The events in a login attempt are captured in web log histories. A good anomaly detector can compare the normal pattern found in the web logs to new and possibly anomalous behavior. The more traces of the events that are left in web logs, the better. For this reason, it can be helpful for the bank to include dynamic security elements that the user must interpret, such as a CAPTCHA, plus image elements that are downloaded.

A dynamic, probabilistic model of the data from the web logs can distinguish the normal and anomalous patterns shown in Figure 6-2. Notice that because the fraud-bot script is forced to use actual image elements from the real bank site on the decoy site, there are in fact two sets of image downloads, plus the two login events (human and bot), on the same timeline. This is *not* a normal pattern, and the anomaly detection model can quickly discover that.

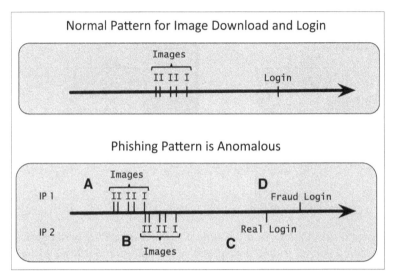

Figure 6-2. The anomaly detection model identifies a potential phishing attack by identifying this anomalous pattern in events on a single timeline for this account. There are two image downloads (events A and B) and two login attempts (events C and D) from different IP addresses along this same timeline.

The model detects the problem and can flag the site that has been hit by suspicious behavior. At this point, human insight and intervention, such as putting a hold on that customer account and notifying the customer that there may have been an attack, is often required. If this happens fast enough, the bot may not be able to steal the funds. That need for rapid response is one reason that building the detector on a system with a realtime file system is important.

How the Model Works

The key here is just like in the previous chapters in that a probabilistic model has to be built that recognizes normal sequences of events. The problem is that the sequences that actually occur are highly varied and often are not recorded as happening quite the way that we might expect. This unexpected result takes place for all kinds of reasons. For instance, most web browsers will only download a limited number of images at the same time. Many browsers will reuse the same TCP connection for many of the image downloads, leading to no overlap. There can also be various forms of caching or load balancing that affect the data we see in the logs. The point is that these differences provide a barrier to building an accurate description manually. What you need is to build a system to read logs and *automatically* build the model based on what *actually* happens, not necessarily based on what you would expect to be the case.

By examining the timelines of many user sessions, the actual patterns of events as represented in the logs can be used to train a model that assigns high probability to event sequences similar to those found in the logs and low probability to sequences that are very different.

One common way to build such a model is to first group all log file events into sessions by browser cookie. Each cookie session is then associated with the user id in any login events in the session. All sessions that reference the same user id are then grouped. This gives a timeline similar to what we saw in Figure 6-2. At this point, all consecutive event pairs in timelines are counted, and the time between events is recorded. These event pairs and times are used to construct a model of plausible event sequences, which in turn gives probabilities for timelines. See the code at *https://github.com/tdunning/sequence-model* for an example of a simple event sequence model.

The log of this probability is an anomaly score just like the anomaly scores that we saw previously in Chapters 4 and 5 for rate or level anomaly detection. This anomaly score can be thresholded using the same adaptive methods using t-digest as described previously.

Putting It All Together

This example of using an anomaly detector to recognize and flag phishing attacks is not only important in its own right as a valuable application of practical machine learning, but it also shows the culmination of all the techniques we have discussed.

The common theme of all these anomaly detectors is that they use a probabilistic model of the data from the past. The log of the probability value that is produced by these models can be used to automatically set a threshold that, when exceeded, sets off an alarm.

The situations that you find yourself in are likely to deviate from the exact patterns that we have described here. The fundamental principle of using a probabilistic model to produce a log probability should apply to your situation as well as it has applied to these examples. Whatever your results are, we would love to hear about them.

CHAPTER 7
Anomaly Detection for the Future

The present is an exciting time for those who are interested in machine learning. The surge of interest in extracting value from growing data sets at large scale has opened up the field for new applications of basic and novel techniques, as well as opened the job market in order to fill the sudden new demand for data scientists and developers experienced with machine learning. The rapid expansion of the use of machine learning in mainstream business operations also means there is increasing importance in designing new, practical approaches that are both approachable and very effective.

These changes also raise the stakes for being able to effectively communicate about these highly technical topics between teams with very different areas of knowledge. This need underlines the usefulness of learning the fundamental concepts and basic approaches to machine learning in order to discuss them in a comprehensible way with decision makers for business solutions, individuals possessing domain knowledge relevant to your project, technical practitioners who more often think in terms of math and code, and newcomers to data science. You must develop the habit of being able to speak of fundamental concepts and methods, using clear and widely understood terms, in order to foster excellent exchanges between these different groups.

With these goals in mind, we also want to look toward the future. Our prediction is that anomaly detection is certainly going to become much more widespread as a basic operation in many aspects of any business or large organization. This increased use of anomaly detection should be especially apparent in the area of interconnected sensors—the Internet of Things that is likely to grow beyond communication with objects to whole system communications, such as manu-facturing or warehousing systems, utility grids, weather-related communications with a variety of other systems including farm equipment or transportation, and so on. As sensors report back to humans or between machines on these complex systems, it will become essential to accurately model expected behavior using approaches that are reasonable to develop and maintain in practical settings. And in addition to understanding expected behavior, it will be important to recognize deviations in a timely manner. That's where anomaly detection comes in. Better data modeling, better compression, storage and access of data, and better training for those who use the data will be the key to making these new systems successful.

In this short publication, we have shown that anomaly detection can be much more than an alarm reacting to a static threshold. These systems can be smart and adaptive. At the same time, we've tried to provide you with the stepping-off points for several simple yet powerful approaches to make anomaly detection practical. As with our previous topic in Practical Machine Learning (*http://www.oreilly.com/data/free/machinelearning.csp*), we are not only providing common ground for expressing complicated ideas, we also are recommending specific approaches that make machine learning accessible and manageable. These approaches take into account real business goals and realistic limitations on resources and consider the benefit of easy and rapid development of machine-learning applications.

In summary, please keep in mind that effective anomaly detection is based on the fundamental concept of modeling what is normal in order to discover what is not. The most effective way to do this is to start with adaptive probabilistic models. One of the very useful practical innovations we have offered you is the freely available algorithm known as *t*-digest, which can be used to accurately measure extreme quantiles and can be applied to both simple and complex models in order to determine appropriate thresholds for anomaly alerts. We discussed the trade-off between sensitive detection of outliers without being overwhelmed by false positives as you do this.

The examples we described graduated from simple noise around a fairly constant value (Chapter 3) to a complex yet repeating pattern for a continuous value (Chapter 4). For an example of the latter, such as an EKG, anomaly detection is accomplished by building a model to predict a normal pattern for a complex curve, making a comparison between that predicted curve (reconstruction curve) and observed measurements in order to determine the reconstruction error. Big spikes in the reconstruction error flag potential anomalies. Similar approaches that use a reconstruction curve and examine reconstruction error to flag anomalies but that employ different techniques to build the model are useful for systems with many measurements at a given time.

Detecting anomalies in systems with sporadic events, such as website traffic, poses a new challenge because counting-based approaches are often not very effective. In Chapter 5, we described systems with sporadic events and explained that the key aspect of the data that is useful to build a model is the arrival time of each event. A good way to measure anomalies in these systems is to multiply the rate you predict for events by the time since the previous event (or *nth* previous event). This product can be used in an analogous way to the use of error calculations from the reconstruction model in the EKG example in Chapter 4.

In Chapter 6 we provide an example that combines many of these concepts in the form of anomaly detection to discover phishing attacks on a secure website.

There is no single way to build an anomaly detector. The choices depend very much on the nature of the system and the need of the architect to accomplish specific goals. But the concepts described here should be helpful in setting you up to tackle your own project as you go in search of the things you don't know to look for.

What remains is for you to decide which mystery you plan to solve…

Additional Resources

GitHub

For the code mentioned in this publication:

Code for t-digest
   https://github.com/tdunning/t-digest

EKG anomaly detection example
   https://github.com/tdunning/anomaly-detection

Simple event sequence model example
   https://github.com/tdunning/sequencemodel

Apache Mahout Open Source Project

The clustering algorithm mentioned in this publication is from Apache Mahout.

For more information on the Apache Mahout project for scalable machine learning, please visit the Mahout website (*https://mahout.apache.org/*). This project welcomes participation. Please feel free to subscribe to the user or developer mailing lists, check the mail archives to see discussions, and follow the community on Twitter at @ApacheMahout (*https://twitter.com/ApacheMahout*).

Additional Publications

To learn how to build a simple but powerful recommendation system, please download *Practical Machine Learning: Innovations in Recommendation* (*http://www.oreilly.com/data/free/machinelearning.csp*), also written by Ted Dunning and Ellen Friedman.

About the Authors

Ted Dunning is Chief Applications Architect at MapR Technologies; committer and PMC member of the Apache Mahout, Apache Zoo-Keeper, and Apache Drill projects; and mentor for these Apache projects: Spark, Storm, Stratosphere, and Datafu. He contributed to Mahout clustering, classification, and matrix decomposition algorithms and helped expand the new version of Mahout Math library. Ted was the chief architect behind the MusicMatch (now Yahoo Music) and Veoh recommendation systems, built fraud-detection systems for ID Analytics (LifeLock), and has issued 24 patents to date. Ted has a PhD in computing science from the University of Sheffield. When he's not doing data science, he plays guitar and mandolin. Ted is on Twitter at @ted_dunning (*https://twitter.com/ted_dunning*).

Ellen Friedman is a consultant and commentator, currently writing mainly about big data topics. She is a committer for the Apache Mahout project and a contributor to the Apache Drill project. With a PhD in Biochemistry, she has years of experience as a research scientist and has written about a variety of technical topics including molecular biology, nontraditional inheritance, and oceanography. Ellen is also co-author of a book of magic-themed cartoons, *A Rabbit Under the Hat*. Ellen is on Twitter at @Ellen_Friedman (*https://twitter.com/ ellen_friedman*).